M000008033

Emotions
for Kids age 1-3
By Dayna Martin

Text © 2015 Dayna Martin
Design © 2015 Engage Books

All rights reserved. No part of this book
may be stored in a retrieval system,
reproduced or transmitted in any form
or by any other means without written
permission from the publisher or a licence
from the Canadian Copyright Licensing
Agency. Critics and reviewers may quote
brief passages in connection with a
review or critical article in any media.

Every reasonable effort has been made
to contact the copyright holders of all
material reproduced in this book.

ENGAGE BOOKS

Mailing address
PO BOX 4608
Main Station Terminal
349 West Georgia Street
Vancouver, BC
Canada, V6B 4A1

www.engagebooks.ca

Written & compiled by: Dayna Martin
Edited & designed by: A.R. Roumanis
Photos supplied by: Shutterstock

FIRST EDITION / FIRST PRINTING

LIBRARY AND ARCHIVES CANADA CATALOGUING IN PUBLICATION

Martin, Dayna, 1983–, author
    Emotions for kids age 1-3 / written by Dayna Martin ; edited by A.R. Roumanis.

(Engage early readers : children's learning books)
Issued in print and electronic formats.
ISBN 978-1-77226-065-6 (paperback). –
ISBN 978-1-77226-066-3 (bound). –
ISBN 978-1-77226-067-0 (pdf). –
ISBN 978-1-77226-068-7 (epub). –
ISBN 978-1-77226-069-4 (kindle)

1. Emotions – Juvenile literature.
I. Roumanis, A. R., editor
II. Title.

BF561.M38 2015   J152.4   C2015-903406-X
                                     C2015-903407-8

Emotions

for Kids age 1-3

Engage Early Readers

Children's Learning Books

By Dayna Martin

ENGAGE BOOKS / VANCOUVER

3

Anger

4

Brave

Love

6

Jealous

Scared

8

Pride

Frustration

Shock

11

Grumpy

12

Shy

13

Annoyed

14

Hope

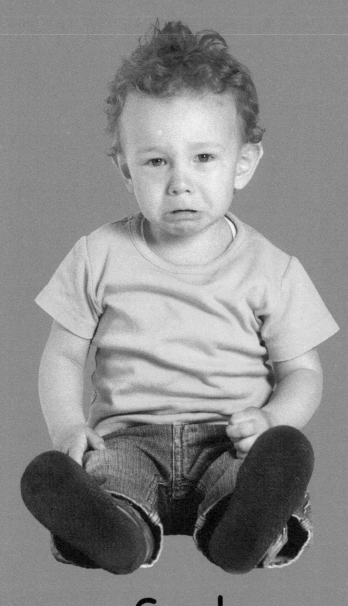

Sad

16

Sleepy

Silly

18

Judgement

Guilt

19

Nervous

20

Pouty

21

Wonder

Surprise

Depressed

24

Disgust

25

Hurt

26

Happy

27

Bored

28

Sorry

Emotions activity

Do you know what these emotions and expressions are called? Can you find **happy, love, surprise, sleepy, scared, anger, brave, sad,** and **shock**? Match the names to the pictures below.

Answer: shock

Answer: scared

Answer: sleepy

Answer: surprise

Answer: brave

Answer: happy

Answer: anger

Answer: sad

Answer: love

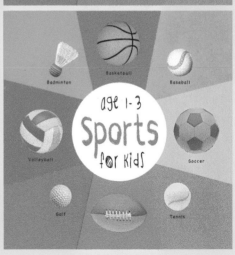

CPSIA information can be obtained
at www.ICGtesting.com
Printed in the USA
BVHW020219250221
601105BV00021B/676

9 781772 260656